MARY AND VINCENT PRICE PRESENT

A NATIONAL TREASURY OF COOKERY

RECIPES OF THE
YOUNG REPUBLIC

Compiled By

HELEN DUPREY BULLOCK

Author of *The Williamsburg Art of Cookery*
Director, Department of Information,
National Trust for Historic Preservation

Illustrated By
CHARLES M. WYSOCKI

HEIRLOOM PUBLISHING COMPANY

Editorial Staff

Coordinating Editor	Robert H. Doherty	*Research Assistants*	Paulette S. Lee
Research Editors	Elvin Abeles		William E. Meyers
	Celia G. Segal		Cory Fox
Home Economists	Eileen Gaden Associates	*Copy Editing and Proofreading*	Ann Henry
	Hazel S. Detwiler		Jason E. Reade
	Nancy Garvey	*Book Design*	Morton Garchik
Picture Research	Shirley L. Green	*Art Associates*	Nicholas Amorosi
	Gabriele Wunderlich		George Geygan

Every recipe in this book has been tested. Occasionally, a particularly interesting old form of a recipe is also included; to distinguish it from the modernized version, the old recipe is given in italic print.

An identifying caption for each full-color picture is printed at the foot of the facing page. A full description of the picture and its source is given in the "List of Full-color Plates" appearing on page 6. Although some pictures are labeled "detail," only slight sections of the picture, in most cases the edges, have not been shown.

Color Separation and Positives by Cyril J. Myatt

Manufactured in the United States of America by Rand McNally & Company

CONTENTS

List of Full-color Plates

Drawings of kitchen utensils by Nicholas Amorosi, staff artist, the American Museum of Natural History, from materials supplied through the courtesy of Colonial Williamsburg, The New-York Historical Society, Shelburne Museum, and Smithsonian Institution.

INTRODUCTION

THE YEARS COVERED IN this book span the birth and adolescence of the young American republic. By 1820 there were almost ten million Americans to enjoy the independence won after two wars. America was extrovert, yet not too confident. Adolescence had set in.

Literature and the arts reflected the lack of confidence. Peale and Stuart depicted patriotic themes but went to school abroad. Benjamin West expatriated himself to England where he presided over the Royal Academy. The writers of the era were little noted nor long remembered, except for Washington Irving, who recalled: "My native country was full of youthful promise. Europe was rich in the accumulated treasures of age."

Among these treasures were kitchen lore. English cook books continued to pour from American presses. *The Compleat Housewife*, after its debut in Williamsburg in 1742, was published from New York in 1764. Susannah Carter's *The Frugal Housewife* appeared in 1772 both in London and in Boston; the later edition was graced by Paul Revere's plates. Came the war; but in 1792 (and for another decade) the Carter anthology continued to help ex-colonials with their kitchen problems. *The Art of Cookery* by Hannah Glasse, the British edition of which had appeared when Washington was a teenager, reached the American scene in 1805. Maria Eliza Rundell's *A New System of Domestic Cookery* went through 67 London editions and almost as many in America from 1806 to 1844.

A true American entry slipped demurely on stage in 1796. Covered in paper, its 48 pages included one detailing errors committed because "the author . . . not having an education sufficient to prepare the work for the press, the person that was employed by her . . . did omit several articles very essential in some of the receipts, and placed others in their stead . . ." Nevertheless, the book had charm, and it *was* a pioneer. Significantly entitled *American Cookery*, and said to be "Adapted to this country, and all grades of life," it was signed by Amelia Simmons, an American orphan. It was reprinted, with added material, until 1822 and made a belated curtain bow (with the author's name) at Woodstock, Vt., in 1831. In 1963 it was recast in the role of a genuine American antique.

Simmons affirmed the American setting. "This treatise is calculated for the improvement of the rising generation of Females in America," the Orphan prefaced. She observed that "the cultivation of Rabbits would be profitable in America, if the best methods were pursued. . . ." Concerning apple culture, she inserted an exhortation to "preserve the orchard from the intrusion of boys, &c. which is not too common in America." And now, at last, melons and "cranberries" and apple pie and three kinds of Indian pudding, to say nothing of an epic on dressing a turtle, appear for the delectation of "American Ladies." The latter continued to favor the English competition, of course, but the offerings in the present volume adopt only those recipes known to be accepted in America in the era of the Young Republic.

As for refrigeration: in 1820 Frederic Tudor of Boston learned how sawdust would insulate ice from the weather, and he shipped the frozen harvest of New England ponds to the West Indies and Southern ports. But for most Americans, ice was where you chopped it. The advice of Amelia Simmons remained relevant: "To have sweet butter in dog days, and thro' the vegetable seasons, send stone pots to honest, neat, and trusty dairy people, and procure it pack'd down in May, and let them be brought in in the night, or cool rainy morning, and partake of no heat from the horse, and set the pots in the coldest part of your celler, or in the ice house."

At long last in the case of the great American drama, the American diet was given a leading role, and while we would never be without foreign supporting players, and why should we since they play their part so well, pride in our native cookery could at last show top billing.

VINCENT PRICE

A SAMPLER OF RECIPES OF THE YOUNG REPUBLIC

THIS OFFERING OF RECIPES in the National Treasury series is neither a primer nor an encyclopedia of American cookery; it is rather a sampler of treasures from the past. Time tested and handed down for generations before they ever became embalmed between the pages of a printed book and reduced to chemical formulas, these recipes are traditional in certain areas and periods, and with groups of different foreign origin. Omissions, beverages, for instance, are conspicuous but deliberate. Tastes in spirituous beverages, for example, have changed substantially since 1738, when Tavern Keeper Henry Wetherburn's "biggest Bowl of Arrack Punch" bought 200 acres of land in Goochland, Virginia, for Thomas Jefferson's father, Peter; or when rum was a staple in the trade of Yankee sailing ships.

But in food, tradition is more persistent. Boston is still the land of the bean and the cod (with many tasty additions); Old New Yorkers can wax emotional over tomatoes in the chowder; and throughout the South there are two mortal sins, trampling on the Confederate flag and putting sugar in the corn bread.

Each recipe in this book has been kitchen tested with modern quantities, but faithfully-chosen ingredients. Detailed instructions are provided. Today's cooks do not have to begin by washing the salt from the butter, cutting sugar from the loaf and pounding it fine and sifting it, nor are most of them able to follow directions that assume the cook knows what to do when told, "add Milk [not saying how much] and put them in the Oven until *enough* [meaning done]." Of course, if they are not *enough*, "do not take them from the Oven or they will be undone and unwholesome." H. D. B.

GUMBO SOUP

2 pounds round steak
½ cup flour
4 to 5 tablespoons butter or margarine
1 large onion chopped
1 quart fresh tomatoes, quartered, or 2 1-pound cans whole tomatoes
2 quarts water
1½ tablespoons salt

¼ teaspoon freshly ground pepper
1 large green pepper, seeded and cut in strips
½ pound fresh whole okra or 1 (10-ounce) package frozen
1 teaspoon tarragon
1 teaspoon thyme
1 bay leaf

Cut the meat in strips 2 inches long, ½ inch wide, and ½ inch thick. Flour the meat and cook in the butter in a Dutch oven until brown. Add the onion and cook until lightly colored. Put in the tomatoes, water, salt, and pepper. Cover and simmer for 1 hour. Add the green pepper, okra, tarragon, thyme, and bay leaf. Cook another hour. Serve in a soup tureen. Makes 10 to 12 servings.

SILVER COFFEE POT BY PAUL REVERE

GRAPE CLUSTER DESSERT MOLD

CHICKEN AND OKRA SOUP

4 slices bacon
1 tablespoon shortening
1 3-pound chicken, cut in
  pieces
2 10-ounce packages frozen
  okra
2 teaspoons salt
4 fresh tomatoes, cut up
1 green pepper, chopped
1 quart boiling water

In a large heavy soup pot or Dutch oven cook the bacon and remove; reserve. Add the shortening to the pot and brown chicken pieces. Add the okra, salt, tomatoes, green pepper, and water. Simmer covered 1 to 1½ hours or till chicken is tender. Correct seasonings. Makes 6 to 8 servings.

CLEAR TOMATO SOUP

7 medium size whole tomatoes
    (or 1 1-pound 12-ounce
    can)
2 pounds beef shin, cut up
1 beef knuckle, split
1 carrot, pared
1 onion, peeled
1 stalk celery
2 sprigs parsley
2 quarts water
1 teaspoon Worcestershire
  sauce
½ teaspoon brown sugar
½ teaspoon salt
⅛ teaspoon pepper
Croutons

In a large kettle combine the tomatoes, shin, bone, carrot, onion, celery, parsley, and water. Bring to a boil; continue to cook stirring and skimming occasionally. Strain; add the Worcestershire, brown sugar, salt, and pepper. Bring to a boil; correct the seasonings. Serve garnished with the croutons. Makes 1 quart, or 4 to 6 servings.

PEA SOUP

2 pounds split peas (1 quart)
1½ pounds lean beef, cut up
½ pound slab bacon, cut up
2 teaspoons powdered mint or
  6 fresh leaves

1 to 2 tablespoons salt
2½ quarts water
2 cups cut-up celery
1 tablespoon celery seed
Croutons

Cover the peas with water and soak overnight. Drain off the water. Place peas in a large soup pot with the beef, bacon, mint, salt, and water. Cook for 3 hours over very low heat. Skim and stir occasionally. Add the celery and celery seed; cook 1 hour longer or until the peas are entirely dissolved and the celery quite soft. This is a very thick soup. You may prefer to add more water to thin it. Strain soup; correct seasonings. Serve with croutons. Makes 10 to 12 servings.

GASPACHO

2 slices toast
4 red-ripe tomatoes, peeled
  and sliced
2 medium-size cucumbers,
  peeled and thinly sliced
¼ cup chopped onion

¼ cup tomato juice
½ teaspoon salt
¼ teaspoon pepper
1 teaspoon prepared mustard
⅛ cup olive oil

Prepare the toast and cut it into small cubes. Prepare the vegetables. Blend together the tomato juice, salt, pepper, mustard, and oil. In 6 soup bowls, arrange a layer of toast cubes, tomato, and cucumber slices. Sprinkle with chopped onion. (Use one fourth of total ingredients allowing for 4 layers.) Drizzle with about one fourth of dressing. Repeat until all ingredients are used. Chill. Makes 6 to 8 generous servings.

BRUNSWICK STEW

4 to 5 pounds pullet, quartered
1½ quarts water
2 slices bacon, cut-up
1 medium onion, sliced
1 (1-pound 12-ounce) can peeled solid pack tomatoes
1 (10-ounce) package frozen kernel corn or 3 ears fresh corn, kernels cut
3 medium potatoes, sliced
1 (10-ounce) package frozen lima beans
Dash cayenne pepper
Salt
½ cup soft bread crumbs

In a Dutch oven or a 6-quart heavy saucepan, cook the chicken in the water with the bacon and onion about 1 hour or until the meat is almost tender. Remove the bones from the chicken and cut into bite-size pieces; return the meat to the Dutch oven. Add the tomatoes, corn, potatoes, beans, and cayenne. Cook until the vegetables and meat are tender. Salt to taste. Just before serving, stir in the bread crumbs. Makes about 6 servings.

PAN

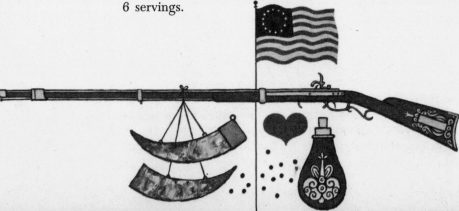

SCALLOPED OYSTERS

24 oysters in shell
1½ cups fine bread crumbs
Butter or margarine

Scrub the oyster shells and open (or have your fish man do this). Arrange the oysters on the half shell in a baking pan. Sprinkle 1 tablespoon of the crumbs on each oyster and dot with butter. Bake in a 375° F. oven about 10 minutes or until the oysters are done and the crumbs tinged with brown. Allow 4 per serving. Makes 6 servings.

CAROLINA DEVILED CLAMS

½ cup chopped celery
½ cup chopped onions
1 chopped green pepper
½ to ¾ teaspoons curry powder
3 tablespoons butter
2 dozen medium clams
   chopped

¾ cup cracker crumbs
2 tablespoons mayonnaise
2 teaspoons Worcestershire
   sauce
3 drops Tabasco sauce
2 eggs well beaten
1 tablespoon lemon juice

Sauté celery, onions, green peppers, and curry in 2 tablespoons of butter until tender. Put the vegetables into a bowl and add clams, ½ cup of the cracker crumbs, mayonnaise, Worcestershire, Tabasco, eggs, and lemon juice. Toss with a fork. Fill 6 ramekins and sprinkle remaining crumbs on the top of each. Dot with remaining butter. Bake in 350° F. oven for 15 minutes until lightly browned. Serves 6.

BAKED SHRIMP AND TOMATO

Beaten Biscuits or crisp, hard crackers

3 tablespoons butter or margarine

1½ pounds shrimp: shelled, deveined, cooked, cut-up or split

Pepper

½ teaspoon mace

1 (1-pound) can stewed tomatoes

Salt

Preheat the oven to 450° F. In a greased 1½-quart baking dish, lay half the biscuits or crackers on the bottom; dot with butter, then put a layer of shrimp, sprinkle with pepper and ¼ teaspoon mace; half of the tomatoes and juice, dot with butter, sprinkle with salt. Repeat layering with shrimp, pepper, mace, butter, the rest of the tomatoes, and sprinkle with salt. Top with the remaining biscuits or crackers, dot with butter. Bake for about 20 minutes or until top is brown. Makes 4 to 6 servings.

BEATEN BISCUITS

3 cups sifted all-purpose flour

½ teaspoon salt

1 tablespoon granulated sugar

½ cup butter or margarine

½ cup milk

In a large mixing bowl, sift flour, salt, and sugar together. Cut in butter until mixture resembles coarse cornmeal. Stir in milk and knead to a smooth dough. Place the dough on a floured board and pound dough with a rolling pin (about 25 minutes).

Dining room, Monticello
Charlottesville, Virginia ▶

As the dough flattens, bring edges to center folding the dough in layers. Preheat oven to 350° F. Roll the dough about ¼ inch thick. Cut out with 1½-inch round biscuit cutter, placed on ungreased baking sheet. With a fork, prick the tops of the biscuits. Bake for 30 minutes or until light golden. Makes about 7 dozen.

FRIED SMELT

1 dozen cleaned large smelt
    (about 1½ to 2 pounds)
¼ cup all-purpose flour
2 egg yolks, well beaten

2 tablespoons cold water
⅓ cup fine dry bread crumbs
1 teaspoon salt
    Fat for frying

Wash the fish, if necessary. Blot dry on paper towels. Dip them in flour, then in combined egg yolks and cold water. Coat well and roll in crumbs. Sprinkle with salt. Heat fat in a large heavy skillet and fry the smelt, turning to brown lightly on both sides. Makes 4 servings.

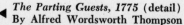

The Parting Guests, 1775 (detail)
By Alfred Wordsworth Thompson

BOILED DUCKS WITH ONION SAUCE

Scald and draw your ducks, put them in warm water for a few minutes, then take them out and put them in an earthen pot; pour over them a pint of boiling milk, and let them lie in it two or three hours; when you take them out, dredge them will with flour, and put them in a copper of cold water; put on the cover, let them boil slowly twenty minutes, then take them out, and smother them with onion sauce. To make onion sauce boil eight or ten large onions, change the water two or three times while they are boiling; when enough, chop them on a board to keep them a good colour, put them in a sauce pan with a quarter of a pound of butter and two spoonsful of thick cream; boil it a little, and pour it over the ducks.

Duckling, about 4½ pounds	Parsley sprigs
Salt	6 medium onions, peeled
All-purpose flour	¼ cup butter or margarine
Few celery leaves	2 tablespoons heavy cream

Rinse the duckling cavity well, drain and pat dry. Sprinkle with salt, dredge the duckling in flour and set in a large saucepan or a Dutch oven, with the celery leaves and parsley sprigs. Add water to cover the duck, bring to a boil, skim the foam from the surface, and simmer about 1½ hours or until tender. Meanwhile, cook the onions in boiling salted water until tender. Drain well, chop the onions and return to the saucepan; add the butter and cream. Serve over the duckling. Makes about 4 servings.

Note: Using "ready-to-cook" frozen, clean, domestic ducklings eliminates the presoaking step.

COFFEE MILL

BEEF A LA MODE

¼ pound fat bacon or salt pork
1 cup vinegar
2 teaspoons salt
½ teaspoon freshly ground
    black pepper
¼ teaspoon ground cloves
1 teaspoon each thyme,
    savory, marjoram
2 teaspoons finely chopped
    parsley

4 to 5 pounds bottom round of
    beef
1 cup chopped onions
2 tablespoons fat
2 carrots, cut in chunks
1 cup turnips, cut in chunks
2 stalks celery, cut in chunks
1 cup water
1 cup port wine

Cut the bacon (or the pork) into slices 1 inch thick; dip them in the vinegar and then into a seasoning mixture of the salt, pepper, cloves, thyme, savory, marjoram, and parsley. With a sharp knife make enough holes in the beef deep enough and wide enough so that you can insert the slices of bacon. Rub the beef with the rest of the seasoning mixture.

In a Dutch oven brown the onions in fat; drain off the fat. Place the meat in the Dutch oven with the carrots, turnips,

SILVER SUGAR BOWL

celery, and water; cover and simmer gently. From time to time turn the meat and gradually add the vinegar. Cook 4 hours or until fork-tender. Remove the meat and the vegetables to a platter. Spoon off fat from the gravy. Add the wine and reheat. Makes 10 to 12 servings.

BEEF HEART STEWED

1 beef heart (about 3 pounds)
  Butter or margarine
2 slices bread
  Pepper
  Salt

1 medium onion, finely
  minced or ½ teaspoon
  dried thyme (optional)
  Hot water
  All-purpose flour

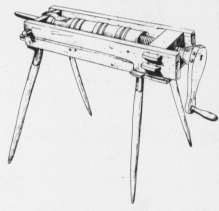

SAUSAGE STUFFER

Cut the fibrous parts out of the top and inside of the heart; wash well and drain. Butter the bread, place in a shallow dish, and sprinkle with pepper, salt, and the onion or thyme, as desired. Add about 3 tablespoons of hot water to moisten the bread. Stuff the heart with the seasoned bread mixture; close the opening with skewers. Place the heart in a heavy saucepan, add 1½ quarts water to cover; cook until tender, about 2 hours. Drain and measure the broth, returning only 1 cup to the saucepan with the meat. Soften ¼-cup butter, dredge in 2 tablespoons flour, stir into the broth in the saucepan. Add ½ teaspoon pepper and 1 teaspoon salt; cover and braise over moderate heat, turning frequently to brown the meat on all sides.

Remove the meat to a serving platter, remove the skewers. Stir 1 cup of hot water into the drippings, bring to boil and pour over the heart. Slice meat to serve. Makes about 6 servings.

SPICED BEEF ROUND

To a large round of beef, take three ounces of saltpetre, finely powdered; rub it well and let it stand five or six hours; then season it highly with common salt, two ounces of pepper and two ounces of allspice, coarsely pounded, and a quarter of a pound of coarse brown sugar. Let it stand in pickle ten or twelve days, turning it now and then. Wash the salt and spice from it, and put it into an earthen pan to bake, with some beef suet. At the top and bottom cover it with a thick paste. Let it bake six or seven hours, if very large. When taken out of the oven, pour the gravy from it, and let it stand until cold. It will keep, in winter, several weeks.

MILK PITCHER

5- to 6-pound bottom round of beef	1 tablespoon allspice
1 teaspoon saltpeter	½ cup brown sugar
½ cup coarse salt	¼ pound beef suet
1 tablespoon pepper	1 cup water
	Pie dough

Rub the beef with saltpeter; refrigerate for 5 or 6 hours, then season with salt, pepper, allspice, and brown sugar. Refrigerate the meat for 10 days, turning occasionally.

Wash the meat. In a large covered baking dish place the suet with the meat on top of it. Pour on the water. Seal the casserole with a strip of dough. Bake in 350° F. oven 3 hours. Pour off the juices; cool. Makes 8 to 10 servings.

CORNED BEEF AND CABBAGE

Boil five pounds of corned or salt beef in five quarts of water, very gently for one hour, and skim it clear, then add two small heads of cabbage cut in quarters and well washed, (examine carefully, as insects are sometimes concealed between the leaves;) then it is done tender, which will be in about forty minutes, take out the largest pieces, and drain them in a cullender, put them in a covered dish, over a pot of boiling water to keep it hot; as soon as the meat is tender, take that up also, (try it by sticking a fork into it, if when you twist the fork the meat breaks, it is enough,) put it between two plates to press, and set it over a pot of hot water to keep hot; add to the soup two or three turnips peeled and slices; one large or two small carrots sliced or grated, and an onion or leek sliced also; six or eight equal sized potatoes peeled neatly; let it boil for half an hour when the vegetables will be done; stir into it a batter made of a tablespoonful of wheat flour and cold water; cover it for ten minutes and it is done.

Then take the potatoes into a dish and serve the soup in a tureen.

LOAF SUGAR GRATER

5 pounds corned beef	2 carrots, scraped and sliced
3 to 5 quarts water	1 onion, sliced
2 or 3 turnips, peeled and sliced	2 small heads of cabbage, quartered
6 to 8 medium-size potatoes, peeled and quartered	1 tablespoon flour

Place the corned beef in a large pot; cover with water; cook about 6 hours or until the meat is tender, adding water as needed.

Kitchen, Tryon Palace
New Bern, North Carolina ▶

Remove the cooked meat to a platter. Add the turnips, potatoes, carrots, and onion to the meat broth. Cook 20 to 30 minutes until the vegetables are tender. Set the cabbage on top 10 minutes before you think the vegetables will be done. Remove the vegetables from the pot; keep warm. Mix flour into a smooth paste with a little water; stir into the broth and cook, stirring a few minutes; season to taste. Serve the broth as a soup. Slice the beef and surround with vegetables. Makes 8 to 10 servings.

BEEF RAGOUT

4 to 4½ pounds rump of beef, cut in 1-inch cubes
¾ cup flour
2 to 3 tablespoons salad oil
1 cup hot water
7 ounces beer (about 1 cup)
1 teaspoon salt
¼ teaspoon pepper
½ teaspoon each parsley flakes and rosemary leaves
¼ teaspoon each savory, majoram, and basil
1 cup carrots
1 cup celery
1 strip of lemon peel 3 inches by 1 inch
1 onion, peeled
8 to 10 whole cloves
2 tablespoons catsup

Coat the beef cubes in flour; brown in hot oil in a Dutch oven. Pour in the water, beer, seasonings, carrots, celery, lemon, and the onion studded with the cloves. Cover and cook gently 1½ hours, stirring occasionally, or until the meat is tender. Remove the onion and stir in catsup. Correct the seasonings. You may add sliced mushrooms, artichoke bottoms boiled and quartered, or hard-cooked egg yolks. Makes 6 servings.

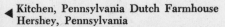

Kitchen, Pennsylvania Dutch Farmhouse
Hershey, Pennsylvania

PLAW

This is generally made of the head, feet, and any pieces which may be left after having made sausage meat.

Scrape and wash well all the pieces designed for the scrapple, put them in a pot with just as much water as will cover them. Add a little salt, and let them boil slowly till the flesh is perfectly soft, and the bones loose. Take all the meat out of the pot, pick out the bones, cut it up fine, and return it to the liquor in the pot. Season it with pepper, salt, and rubbed sage, to the taste. Set the pot over the fire, and just before it begins to boil, stir in gradually as much Indian meal as will make it as thick as thick mush. Let it boil a few minutes, take it off, and pour it in pans. When cold, cut it in slices, flour it, and fry it in hot lard, or sausage fat.

2½ pounds veal cutlet, in one piece
1 quart water
1 teaspoon salt
½ teaspoon pepper
½ to 1 teaspoon curry powder
½ teaspoon parsley flakes
2 tablespoons butter or margarine
1 cup raw regular rice

Place the meat in a soup pot or Dutch oven; cover with water; add salt and pepper. Simmer, covered, 1 hour or until the meat is fork tender. Remove the meat from the broth and cut into ½-inch-thick strips 3 or 4 inches long. Measure the liquid and add water if necessary to make 3 cups. To the liquid in the pot add the curry, parsley, butter, and rice. Bring the liquid to a boil, then lower the heat and cook 10 minutes. Add the cut-up meat and cook 5 to 10 minutes longer. The rice should be tender and very little liquid left. Makes 4 servings.

SCRAPPLE

1½ pounds boneless pork
Water
2 teaspoons salt
½ teaspoon pepper
1 teaspoon ground sage
1 cup yellow cornmeal
Bacon fat

In a 3-quart saucepan, place the meat with water to cover and salt; cook about 2 hours, until the meat is very tender. Remove the meat, measure the broth and add water if necessary to make 3 cups of liquid. Mince the meat very fine, and return with the broth to the saucepan. Add the pepper and sage. Mix the cornmeal with 1 cup of cold water, then stir into the meat and broth. Cook over low heat until thickened, stirring frequently. Then cover and continue cooking over low heat for 10 minutes longer. Rinse a 9- x 5- x 3-inch loaf pan with cold water. Turn the cornmeal mixture into the pan. Chill well. Unmold and cut into ½- to ¾-inch slices; flour them and brown slowly in hot bacon fat. Makes about 6 to 8 servings.

SHOW THE CORN
TOOT THE HORN
LOVES TO ROAM
GET HIM HOME

SUCCOTASH

Take of dried sweet corn and white beans—one quart of dried sweet corn, to one or two of beans.

Put the beans to soak in a basin, with water to cover them; rinse the corn in a basin with water to cover it, let them remain until the next day; within two hours of dinner time, pour the water from the beans, pick out any imperfections, and put them with the corn, with the water in which it is soaked, into a dinner-pot; cut a pound of nicely corned pork in thin slices, put it to the corn and beans, and put over them hot water, rather more than to cover them; add a very small red pepper, or a saltspoonful of cayenne, and cover the pot close; set it where it will boil very gently, for an hour and a half, then put it in a deep dish; add a bit of butter to it and serve.

½ pound dried lima beans
   (about 1¼ cups)
¼ pound salt pork, sliced
   ½-inch thick

½ teaspoon cayenne pepper
½ teaspoon salt
Water
1 can (12-ounce) kernel corn

Soak the beans overnight, then drain. Place the salt pork on the bottom of a Dutch oven or heavy sauce pan; Add the beans, pepper, salt, and water to cover. Simmer for 1½ hours or until beans are tender, stirring occasionally and adding more water if needed. Just before serving stir in the corn, serve hot with salt pork. Makes 1 quart or 8 servings.

POTATOES IN CREAM

1 tablespoon butter or
    margarine
1 tablespoon flour
½ teaspoon salt
⅛ teaspoon pepper

1 tablespoon minced onion
1 cup heavy cream
1 quart sliced potatoes,
    cooked
1 teaspoon chopped parsley

In a large saucepan melt the butter then mix in the flour, salt, and pepper to make a smooth paste. Stir in the onion and cream. Cook stirring until the mixture is smooth and thickened. Add the potatoes and continue to cook until the potatoes are heated through; sprinkle on the parsley. Makes 6 servings.

CORN CASSEROLE

6 ears of corn
4 eggs
1 tablespoon cream

¾ teaspoon salt
⅛ teaspoon pepper
1 teaspoon sugar

Cook the corn in boiling salted water till tender; drain. Cut the corn from the cob (about 3 cups). Separate the eggs. Combine the yolks, cream, salt, pepper, sugar, and corn. Beat the whites until they form stiff peaks. Fold whites into the corn mixture. Pour into a well-greased 1½ quart casserole. Bake in 425° F. oven 20 minutes or until puffy and golden. Makes 6 servings.

EGGS AND TOMATOES

3 tablespoons butter
1 tablespoon finely chopped
   onion
3 large red-ripe tomatoes,
   skinned and coarsely diced

¾ teaspoon salt
¼ teaspoon pepper
3 eggs, well beaten

Melt the butter in a large, heavy skillet. Add the onion and cook for 2 minutes or until the onion is transparent. Add the tomatoes, salt, and pepper. Cook, stirring frequently, for 5 to 6 minutes or until the tomato pulp can be easily mashed. Mash slightly. Stir in the beaten eggs and continue to cook, stirring occasionally, for 2 minutes, or until the eggs are set. Makes 4 to 5 servings.

Kitchen, Nathan Hale Homestead
Coventry, Connecticut ▶

GERMAN WAFFLES

A pint of the richest cream, four eggs, half a gill of yeast, a little salt, and flour enough to make a batter as thick as for griddle cakes. The waffle iron must be heated on hot coals and then buttered, one side filled with batter, shut up and laid upon the coals; in a few minutes, turn it upon the other side. These cakes may also be baked excellently on a soapstone griddle rubbed with salt.

1 envelope granular yeast	4 eggs, well beaten
¼ cup warm (not hot) water	1½ teaspoons salt
2 cups heavy cream	3½ cups all-purpose flour

Sprinkle the yeast over warm water. Heat the cream until it is lukewarm and put into a mixing bowl. Stir the yeast until dissolved and blend into the warm cream. Stir in the eggs, salt, and half of the flour. Beat the mixture until smooth. Add the remaining flour, about ½ cup at a time, beating smooth after each addition. Let the batter stand in a warm place (about 85° F.) for ½ hour or until bubbly on top. Heat the waffle iron as the manufacturer directs. Bake the waffles. Makes about 4 to 5 cups batter or enough for 8 waffles.

Wonders—
1/4 ℔ sugar, 1/4 ℔ butter, 3 eggs,
as much flour as it will take in
Roll thin & fry —

◀ Dining room, Gunston Hall
Lorton, Virginia

JARS, JUGS, BOTTLES AND CROCKS ★ ★ ★ ★
SQUARE-HEAD NAILS AND GRANDFATHER CLOCKS
CHICKENS, COWS, HORSES AND PIGS ★ ★ ★ ★ ★
PLUMS, PUMPKINS, APPLES AND FIGS ★ ★ ★ ★
JOYS FROM THE FARM WE LOVE ALL YEAR ★
THIS IS OUR HOME, SMALL AND DEAR. ★ ★ ★ ★

Facsimile of a page from an old manuscript recipe book.

BUCKWHEAT GRIDDLE CAKES

1 envelope granular yeast	¼ teaspoon baking soda
3 cups lukewarm water	2 cups buckwheat flour
1½ teaspoons salt	½ cup white cornmeal

Sprinkle the yeast over the warm water in a bowl. Blend together the salt, soda, buckwheat flour, and cornmeal. Stir about half of the flour mixture into the water with yeast. Beat until smooth. Add the remaining flour and beat again until mixture is smooth and blended. Let stand for about ½ hour in a warm place (about 85° F.), free from drafts or until the surface of the batter is bubbly. Beat again. Heat griddle; grease lightly and fry the cakes, using about 3 tablespoons batter for each. Turn to brown both sides. If batter thickens, add a little milk if necessary. Cakes should be about the thickness of a silver dollar. Serve with butter and maple syrup. Makes about 20 to 24 2½-inch cakes or enough to serve 6.

MRS. MADISON'S WHIM

6 eggs, separated
1 pound butter or margarine, softened
2 cups granulated sugar
¼ cup brandy
1 teaspoon nutmeg

4 cups sifted cake flour
½ teaspoon baking soda
1 tablespoon hot water
1 (11-ounce) package raisins, floured (with ¼ cup flour)

Preheat oven to 300° F. In a medium bowl, whip the egg whites until stiff. In a large mixing bowl, cream the butter; gradually add the sugar, then the egg yolks.

Beat well, add the brandy and nutmeg. Blend in the flour. Dissolve the soda in hot water, stir into the batter; add the raisins, mix well. Gently fold in the egg whites. Turn into 2 (1½-quart) loaf baking dishes (8- x 5- x 2-inches) or 1 (3-quart) tube pan. Bake in a slow oven for 1½ to 2 hours, or until a cake tester inserted in the center of the cake comes out clean. Makes 1 large tube cake or 2 small loaf cakes.

MORAVIAN SUGAR CAKE

¼ pound butter or margarine (½ cup)	1 egg, well beaten
2 cups warm milk	1 teaspoon oil of cinnamon or powdered cinnamon
1 package active dry yeast	¼ cup soft butter or margarine
¼ cup warm water	1 cup brown sugar
6 cups sifted all-purpose flour	2 teaspoons cinnamon
1 teaspoon salt	2 teaspoons granulated sugar

Dissolve ¼ pound butter in the warm milk. Sprinkle the yeast over the warm water; let stand a few minutes to dissolve. Place 4 cups of the flour and the salt in a large bowl; make a well in the center. Pour the milk mixture and yeast into the well; stir to mix well. Cover the bowl and set in a warm place to rise, about 2 hours. When the dough has risen and is bubbly stir in the egg, remaining flour, and oil of cinnamon. Put the dough in a well-greased 9- x 9- x 3-inch square pan; set to rise again. When the batter has doubled in bulk combine the remaining butter, brown sugar, and cinnamon into a smooth paste. With a knife make gashes all over the top of the cake. With a spoon fill each gash with some of the brown sugar mixture and pinch or push dough over the sugar mixture to be sure it won't run out. Sprinkle the top of the cake with granulated sugar. Bake in 375° F. oven about 40 minutes or until the top is golden brown; cool 10 minutes; remove from the pan onto a wire rack. Cut the cooled cake into 9 to 12 servings.

COCONUT MACAROONS

3 egg whites
2 cups sifted confectioners' sugar
3 to 4 cups fine grated coconut

Beat the egg whites till very frothy, then beat in the sugar and continue beating until the mixture is very stiff. Snip or chop the coconut very fine. Stir the coconut into the egg-white mixture to form a very stiff paste. With floured hands very gently roll a tablespoonful at a time into small balls. Place a few inches apart on a greased cookie sheet. Bake in 425° F. oven 8 to 10 minutes. Remove from the pan at once. Makes about 4½ dozen.

JUMBLES

Grate a large cocoa-nut. Rub half a pound of butter into a pound of sifted flour, and wet it with three beaten eggs, and a little rose water. Add by degrees the cocoa-nut, so as to form a stiff dough. Flour your hands and your paste-board, and dividing the dough into equal portions, make the jumbles with your hands into long rolls, and then curl them round and join the ends so as to form rings. Grate loaf-sugar over them; lay them in buttered pans, (not so near as to run into each other,) and bake them in a quick oven from five to ten minutes.

¼ pound butter or margarine (½ cup)	½ cup finely grated coconut
2 cups sifted all-purpose flour	½ teaspoon rose water (optional)
2 eggs, well beaten	Granulated sugar

With a pastry blender or 2 knives scissors-fashion blend the butter into the flour. Blend in the eggs, coconut, and rose water to form a stiff dough. Pinch off a lump about a tablespoonful at a time. Roll lumps of dough between the palms of your hand to form a rope about 4 inches long and ½ inch wide. Form into a ring; sprinkle with sugar. Bake on a well-greased cookie sheet in 450° F. oven 10 minutes or until tinged with brown. Remove at once to a wire rack. Makes 2½ dozen.

LATE EATING OF JUMBLES
MAY BRING MIDNIGHT RUMBLES

Facsimile of a page from an old manuscript recipe book.

Gingerbread
1/2 flour 1/2 # sugar 1/2 # butter, 3 eggs
1 gill cream — pearlash & ginger

Cider Cake —
2 # flour, 1/2 # butter, 1/2 #, sugar, 1 pt

HARD GINGERBREAD

To three quarters of a pound of treacle beat one egg strained; mix four ounces of brown sugar, half an ounce of ginger sifted, of cloves, mace, allspice and nutmeg, a quarter of an ounce, beaten as fine as possible; coriander and carraway seeds, each a quarter of an ounce; melt one pound of butter, and mix with the above; and add as much flour as will knead into a pretty stiff paste; then roll it out, and cut into cakes.

Bake on tin plates in a quick oven. A little time will bake them.

Of some, drops may be made.

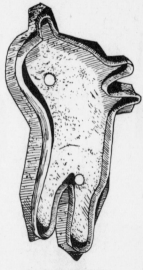

COOKIE CUTTER

1½ cup molasses
1 egg, beaten
½ cup brown sugar
1 teaspoon ground ginger
½ teaspoon each ground cloves,
    mace, allspice, nutmeg
½ teaspoon each coriander
    seeds and caraway seeds
    (optional)

1 pound butter or margarine,
    melted
About 2 pounds (8 cups)
    all-purpose flour

In a large bowl, combine the molasses with egg, then add the brown sugar and spices. Add the melted butter. Add the flour gradually, then knead into a stiff dough. Wrap in waxed paper. Chill. Preheat the oven to 375° F. Roll out ¼ of the dough at a time on a floured board and cut out gingerbread men or other shapes as desired. Bake on ungreased baking sheets for about 10 minutes, depending on thickness of the dough. Makes about 7 dozen (5-inch) gingerbread men.

BOURBON AND BLACK WALNUT CAKE

DAGGER

2 cups white sugar	¼ teaspoon salt
2¼ cups brown sugar, firmly packed	1 teaspoon freshly grated nutmeg
1½ cups butter (3 sticks)	1 pint 100-proof bourbon whiskey
6 eggs	1 pound black walnut meats
5½ cups all-purpose flour, sifted	

Mix the white and brown sugar until free from lumps. Cream the butter in a large mixing bowl and add half the sugar mixture. Cream thoroughly. Then cream some more. This will govern the texture of your cake. In a separate bowl beat the eggs until light and fluffy, and add the remaining sugar. Stir into the butter mixture. Sift the flour, salt, and nutmeg and add to the batter, alternating with the whiskey, beginning and ending with the flour. Add the walnut meats, but do not bother to fold; a little extra beating will tend to bruise the walnuts, releasing the oil and flavor into the cake. Pour into a well-greased and floured 10-inch tube pan or, if you prefer smaller cakes, into 4 small loaf pans. Bake in a 300° F. oven for 1½ to 2 hours for the large cake, or 1¼ hours for the smaller ones, or until the cake shrinks slightly from the sides of the pan. Remove from the oven and allow to stand for 15 minutes, then turn out on a cake rack. When completely cool, wrap in foil and store in the refrigerator. Do not freeze. The crust of this cake will be rather hard and dry, and the inside should have a moist texture.

Kitchen, Van Cortlandt Manor House
Croton-on-Hudson, New York

RHUBARB CHESS PIE

9–inch prebaked pie shell
1 tablespoon butter
1 cup sugar
¼ cup flour
2 eggs

1 cup fresh rhubarb, cut in
  ½-inch pieces
1 cup milk
¼ teaspoon salt
¼ teaspoon nutmeg

Cream together the butter and sugar. Add the flour. Separate the eggs. Beat the yolks and add to the remaining ingredients. Beat the whites until stiff but not dry and mix gently with the other ingredients. Pour into the pie shell and bake at 350° F. for 45 minutes. The shell may be baked for 5 minutes before the filling is added—an insurance against sogginess.

Mince meat for Pies—
1 ℔ of meat, 3/4 of suet, 1 ℔
raisins, 1 ℔ sugar, 1 oz cloves
1 oz of cinnamon, the weight
of the whole in apples, &
a pint of wine or cider.

Facsimile of a page from an old manuscript recipe book.

◀ Kitchen, Ford Mansion
Morristown, New Jersey

SHAKER STOVE

APPLE PIE

Pare, quarter, and core the apples; cut them into thin bits. Put into the bottom of a pie-dish a tablespoonful of brown sugar, with a tea-spoonful of grated ginger and lemon-peel, then a layer of apples, and so on alternately, till the dish is piled as full as it will hold. The next day, wet the rim of the dish, line it with puff or tart paste, brush it with water, and cover it with paste; press the edge all around, notch it with a paste-cutter, and make a small hole with the point of a knife in the middle. It may be seasoned with two table-spoonfuls of lemon or orange marmalade, pounded cinnamon, mace, and cloves, in addition to the ginger and lemon-peel.

POTATO MASHER

2 tablespoons brown sugar
2 teaspoons grated lemon rind
2 teaspoons ground ginger
1 teaspoon cinnamon
½ teaspoon mace
¼ teaspoon ground cloves

2 tablespoons orange
   marmalade
2 pounds greening or other
   pie apples
Pastry for 9-inch pie shell

Combine the brown sugar, rind, spices, and marmalade, and sprinkle half of it in the bottom of a deep-dish pie plate (9 inches in diameter and 2 inches deep). Pare, quarter, and slice the apples thin (about 6 cups). Put half of the apples in the dish; repeat layering with the rest of the spice combination and the apples. Cover the dish with waxed paper and refrigerate.

Roll the pastry into a circle slightly larger than the pie plate. Fit the pastry onto the top of the pie. In the middle of the pastry make a small hole with the point of a knife; notch the edges. Bake in 425° F. oven for 40 minutes, or until the apples are tender. Makes 6 to 8 servings.

APPLE PANDOWDY

10 large apples	½ cup light molasses
½ cup sugar	¼ cup water
½ teaspoon cinnamon	3 tablespoons melted butter
¼ teaspoon nutmeg	Pastry for 9-inch pie shell
Dash salt	

Make a pie crust as usual and roll out. Brush with melted butter, and cut in half. Fold over, and repeat the operation. This makes a very flaky pastry. Chill while peeling the apples.

Peel, core, and slice apples into thin pieces. Mix the sugar, spice, and salt, and combine with apple slices; place in a baking dish. Combine the molasses, water, and melted butter, and pour over apples. Cover with pastry. Cook in a 400° F. oven for 10 minutes; then turn heat down to 325° F. and cook for 30 minutes, or until pastry begins to brown and the apples are juicy. At this point remove from the oven and "dowdy" the crust by cutting through crust and apples with a sharp knife. Return to the oven for another 10 minutes. Serve warm with cream or ice cream. Six to eight servings.

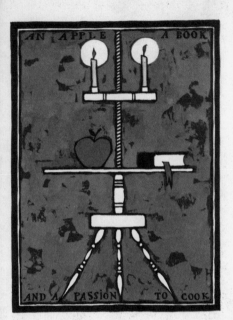

Facsimile of a page from an old manuscript recipe book.

Apple Pudding —
1 ℔ sifted apples, ½ ℔ sugar, 9 eggs, ¼ ℔ butter, 1 qt sweet milk, 1 gill rose water, some cinnamon 2 rusk soaked in wine, a green lemon pe grated, put on paste no 7 —

A BOUNTIFUL YEAR IS SUCH A DELIGHT
AND NO NEED TO CURB THE APPETITE

TIPSY CAKE

6–inch sponge cake layer
¼ cup brandy
¼ cup white wine
1 to 2 tablespoons
    confectioners' sugar

Custard based on 2 cups
    milk or cream
Blanched almonds

Put the cake into a 9-inch pie plate or serving dish. Sprinkle the combined brandy and wine over the cake; let it soak up a few minutes. Sprinkle the sugar over the cake; pour on the custard; refrigerate. Garnish with split or chopped almonds. Makes 6 to 8 servings.

Put a sponge-cake into a deep glass dish, pour around it a glass of brandy and some raisin-wine, and let it soak it up; then strew sifted sugar over it, pour a thick custard into the dish, and ornament the top with blanched almonds split and put thick.

Blanc Manger.

4. oz. sweet almonds, with 5. or 6 bitter
almonds. pour boiling water on them
to take off the skin.
put them in a mortar & beat them
with a little cream.   delayer
take them out of the mortar & liquefy
them with cream little by little (near a
pint) stirring them.
4. oz. sugar not to be put in.
have ready some
                   isinglass (colle de poisson)
say 1. oz. dissolved in boiling water & pour it
into the preceding mixture,
stirring them well together.
strain it thro' a napkin.
put it into a mould, & it is done.

Vine jellies.

take 4. calves feet & wash them well
without taking off the hoofs. (or in-
-stead of that 1. oz. isinglass, or 1. oz.
of deershorns)
these feet must be well boiled the
day before they are wanted.
let them cool in order to take off the grease
after taking off the grease put the jelly
in a casserole. put there 4 oz. sugar
cloves, nutmeg. boil all together.
take 6. whites of eggs, the juice of 6 le-
-mons, a pint of milk, a pint of madeira
stir all together.
pour it into the jelly & boil it.
strain the whole thro' flannel.
taste it to see if sweet enough, if
not, add powdered sugar.
strain it 2 or 3 times thro' flan-
-nel till clear.
put it in glasses or moulds.

Macaroons

pour boiling water on you
    almonds & take off [...]
put wash them in cold wate
wipe them well in a towel
beat them
and whites of eggs from tim   to tim
    beating them always to
    prevent their turning into
    oil.
take them out of the mortar
add sugar & whites of eggs.
beat them well with a wood-
    -en spoon.
taste the paste to see
    if it is not too bitter
add sugar if you find it too b[...]
dresser les avec deux cont[...]
    le grosseur d'un noia[...]
    des feuilles de papier.
put them in an oven not too [...]
    but hotter than after taking
    out the bread.
you prove the proper heat of [...]
    oven by holding in it a lit[...]
    white paper. if it burns, it [...]
    burn your macaroons, if [...]
    just browns the paper it i[...]
    exact.

ALBEMARLE PEACH CHUTNEY

1 quart peeled and sliced peaches
½ cup cider vinegar
1½ cups dark brown sugar
2 tablespoons grated onion
1 cup diced, peeled apple
½ cup seedless raisins
1 teaspoon mustard seed
2 teaspoons ginger
½ teaspoon salt
1 teaspoon cumin powder
1 teaspoon grated lemon rind
1 tablespoon lemon juice

In a heavy pot place the peaches and rest of the ingredients. Cook slowly, stirring until the ingredients are well blended. Continue to cook until the mixture is soft and thickened. Pack into sterilized jars while hot and seal. Makes 3 cups.

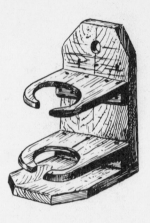

ASPARAGUS BUNCHER

Good food Good drink

17 95

Good feLLowshiP

PISTACHIO CREAM

Take out the kernels of half a pound of pistachio nuts, and beat them in a mortar with a spoonful of brandy. Put them into a pan with a pint of good cream, and the yolks of two eggs beat fine. Stir it gently over the fire till it grows thick, and then put it into a china soup-plate. When it is cold, stick it over with small pieces of the nuts, and send it to table.

½ pound shelled pistachio nuts   2 cups light cream
1 tablespoon brandy   3 egg yolks, well beaten

Reserve a few whole nuts for garnish. Grind the rest, or pulverise them in the blender. In a small saucepan blend together the nuts and brandy. Combine the cream and beaten egg yolks; Stir into the nuts. Cook over low heat, stirring constantly, until mixture thickens and bubbles around the edges of the pan. Remove from the heat at once: Pour into a bowl; cover, and chill. Serve topped with bits of the reserved pistachio nuts. Makes 4 servings.

CERAMIC PUNCH POT

*A sick bed custard —
Scald a qt of milk, sweeten & salt a little, whip 3 eggs & stir in, Bake on coals in a proper vessel —*

Facsimile of a page from an old manuscript recipe book.

TANSEY

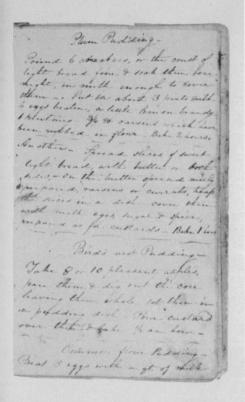

Beat seven eggs, yolks and whites separately: add a pint of cream, near the same of spinachjuice, and a little tanseyjuice gained by pounding in a stonemortar; a quarter of a pound of Naples biscuit, sugar to taste, a glass of white wine, and some nutmeg. Set all in a saucepan, just to thicken, over the fire; then put into a dish, line with paste to turn out and bake it.

6 eggs, separated
1 pint heavy cream
½ cup granulated sugar
½ cup white wine or sherry
¼ pound Naples biscuit (or lady fingers) broken up

¼ teaspoon nutmeg
Few drops green food coloring (optional)
1 pastry-lined 10-inch pie plate

Place the egg yolks in a saucepan and beat slightly. Stir in the cream, sugar, and sherry, and add the biscuits and the nutmeg. Cook stirring until the mixture thickens. Add the green coloring if desired. Beat the egg whites until they form stiff peaks and fold in the hot cream mixture. Pour into the pastry-lined pie plate. Bake at 450° F. for 10 minutes, then reduce the heat to 350° F. and bake for 30 minutes longer. The pie will be puffy and golden. Cool on a wire rack. The pie will sink somewhat as it cools. Makes 8 servings.

Facsimile of a page from an old manuscript recipe book.

T a n a C E T u M   V u L G A R E

APHABETICAL LIST OF RECIPES